THE FIRST MIRACLES

William Collins Sons & Co. Ltd
London · Glasgow · Sydney · Auckland
Toronto · Johannesburg

First published in Great Britain in 1990 by Collins Religious Division
part of the Collins Publishing Group
8 Grafton Street, London W1X 3LA

ISBN 0 00 215317-3

Printed and bound in Italy by L.E.G.O.

THE FIRST MIRACLES

by Rachel Billington
and Barbara Brown

COLLINS

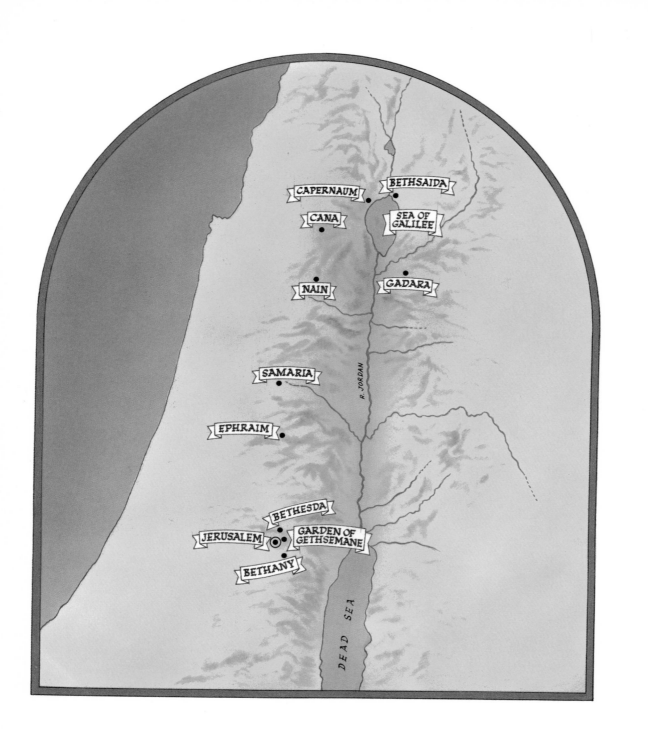

CAPERNAUM

BETHSAIDA

CANA

SEA OF
GALILEE

NAIN

GADARA

SAMARIA

R. JORDAN

EPHRAIM

BETHESDA

JERUSALEM

GARDEN OF
GETHSEMANE

BETHANY

DEAD SEA

THE FIRST miracle of all was Jesus' birth. Mary was his mother but he had no human father, although God was his heavenly father. As a baby, Jesus was honoured by poor shepherds and also rich and wise kings but he grew up as any other little boy. He lived with Mary and his foster father, Joseph, who was a carpenter. It was only when he was thirty years old that he left home and began teaching. On his travels round the Holy Land he also performed a great many miracles so that people knew he was not just another prophet or teacher but truly the son of God.

JESUS' first miracle took place in a village called Cana. It was only a small place, set high in the hills and criss-crossed with rough stone walls enclosing rows of vines and flat-roofed houses with open courtyards. Jesus was invited with two or three of his friends to a wedding party. It was the sort of party that goes on for several days, and when Jesus arrived his mother was already there. She had just noticed that the wine which was being served was running out. Mary turned to her son and asked if he could do anything to help.

Jesus said, "Woman," which was more polite then than it sounds now, "why should I get involved? This isn't the right moment to show who I am."

But his mother knew better and knew too he wouldn't refuse her. So she told the servants, "Do anything he asks you".

In the courtyard there stood six earthenware urns, each big enough to hold at least twenty gallons of water; they were usually used for washing. Jesus told the servants, "Fill the urns with water". And they filled them up to the brim. Then he told them to pour out a cupful and take it to the master of ceremonies.

The master of ceremonies drank what should have been water and found out it had turned into wine. He had no idea where it came from and was astonished at the wonder-ful taste. He called over the bridegroom and said, "Most people serve the best wine first and save the less good until everyone's already had several drinks. But you have saved the best wine for the end of the party!"

The servants who had seen what Jesus had done were amazed, and soon the news of the miracle had spread all round the area. Reluctantly or not, Jesus was on the way to becoming famous.

JESUS left Cana and went south to the city of Jerusalem where he met many people and taught them. But he was back in Cana again when he performed his second miracle. An officer in the royal service lived in Capernaum which is about ten miles away on the shores of a big lake called the Sea of Galilee. His son had fallen sick and indeed was on the point of death.

The officer rode up to Cana and looked for Jesus. When he found him, he begged Jesus to follow him down and heal his son. "He will die very soon", he said miserably.

Jesus did not move. "Will none of you believe unless you see signs and wonders?" he asked reproachfully.

But the officer would not be put off, "Master, come down with me before my child dies."

Then Jesus took pity on him, "Go off now," he said, "your son will live." The officer believed him and started his journey home. Just before he arrived on the following morning, his servants came running out to meet him. "Your son is alive!" they shouted. "He is alive and well!"

"When did he start to get better?" asked the happy father.

"The fever left him yesterday at one o'clock", they explained excitedly. Now it was precisely one o'clock when Jesus had told him, "Your son will live", so he and all his household became Christian believers.

FROM THAT day Jesus cured many people who were sick
from all kinds of different diseases. One morning as he
stood by the Sea of Galilee and the people were crowding
about him to hear his teaching, he noticed two boats lying at
the water edge. The fishermen had come ashore and were
washing their nets. He got into one of the boats, which
belonged to Simon Peter, and asked him to push out a little
way from the shore. Then he continued to talk to the
crowds from his seat in the boat.

When he had finished speaking, he said to Simon Peter, "Put out into deep water and let down your nets for a catch."

"But master," objected Simon Peter, "we have been hard at work all night and caught nothing. Still, if you really want me to, I will let down the nets." So they flung the nets over the sides and soon had caught so many fish that the nets began to split. Then they beckoned over the fishermen from the other boat and between them they loaded both boats so full so that they were nearly sinking.

Simon Peter was surprised and frightened at this miracle and knelt at Jesus' feet, saying "Go, Lord, leave me, for I am a sinner." His partners, two brothers called James and John, were equally astonished.

But Jesus calmed them. "Do not be afraid," he said, "from now on you will be fishers of men."

All three understood he wanted them to join him in his teaching, so when they had safely brought the ships to shore, they left everything and followed Jesus.

ALTHOUGH Jesus spent a lot of time in the country area called Galilee, he also visited Jerusalem regularly, even though it meant several days' walking. Once he was near a pool in a part of the city called Bethesda. Around the water were five archways in which the blind and the lame and the paralysed gathered, for there was a tradition that an angel came to ruffle the waters and that the first person who bathed after this would be cured. One man had lain there waiting for thirty-eight years.

Jesus saw him and said, "Do you want to be cured?"

The man answered, "Sir, I have no one to help me to get into the water so someone else always gets there first."

Jesus said, "Stand up, pick up your stretcher and walk."

The man recovered at once and did what he was told. Soon, however, he was stopped by Jews. They were angry that he was carrying his stretcher on the sabbath, which was a day of rest. He explained, "The man who cured me told me to." They wanted to know who was this man but Jesus had slipped away in the crowd.

However a little later the cured man saw Jesus again in the temple and pointed him out to the Jews. Then Jesus warned him that if he behaved like that, he would become something worse than a cripple. And Jesus defended his behaviour to the Jews, "My father who is God doesn't stop working on the sabbath day so neither shall I."

This made the Jews even more furious because they would not accept that Jesus was God's son.

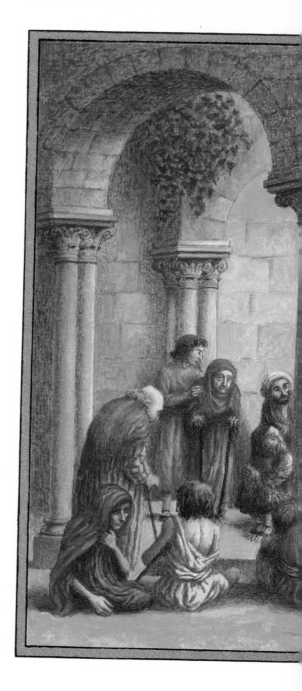

WHEN Jerusalem had become too dangerous or the crowds were too great Jesus retired again to Galilee where he had more friends. He travelled round and taught, even in the smallest villages. But sooner or later, wherever he was, he was discovered and asked to perform miracles.

One day he was preaching in a house at Capernaum to a really enormous crowd. There were so many people that, as he was inside the house, the doorway was completely blocked. Then along the path came four men carrying a paralysed man on a stretcher. They wanted Jesus to cure the sick man but they could not get anywhere near him. So they opened up the roof above his head and lowered the stretcher through the hole.

When Jesus realized the strength of their belief in him, he said to the paralysed man, "My son, your sins are forgiven".

Some lawyers sitting there were shocked. "Why does the fellow talk like this?" they whispered to each other. "This is blasphemy. Only God can forgive sins."

Jesus knew perfectly well what they were thinking and he asked them, "Is it easier to say 'Your sins are forgiven' or 'Stand up, take hold of your bed and walk'? However, in order to convince you that the son of man has the right to forgive sins on earth, I will now say to him, 'Stand up, take hold of your bed and walk'."

At once the sick man picked up his stretcher and walked out of the house, in full view of the astonished crowds.

ALTHOUGH Jesus came from a poor family, his fame was spreading even among the rich and the rulers of his country. A Roman centurion had a servant of whom he was very fond and who was ill. Hearing about Jesus, the centurion sent some Jewish elders to ask Jesus to save his servant's life. "The centurion deserves this favour," they said persuasively, "because he loves our nation and it is he who built us our synagogue."

So Jesus went along with them. But when they were nearing the house, the centurion sent some friends with a message. "Do not trouble to come any further for I am not worthy to receive you under my roof. But only say the word and my servant will be healed. I understand how a word of command works because I am a soldier and I command soldiers. I say to one, 'Go' and he goes, to another 'Come here' and he comes; and to my servant, 'Do this' and he does it."

Jesus was most impressed when he heard this and turned to his followers, "I tell you, I haven't found such faith as this anywhere in Israel."

The messengers returned to the centurion's house and found the servant quite recovered.

From Capernaum, Jesus travelled to a town called Nain. When he came near the gates, a dead man was carried out on a bier. He was the only son of a widow who was weeping at his side, accompanied by many people from the town.

Jesus saw all this and felt very sorry for her. "Stop crying now", he said, and he stepped forward and put his hands on the bier so that the bearers stood still. Then he spoke, "Young man, rise up!" The dead man sat up and began to speak.

QUITE OFTEN Jesus taught by the lakeside; it was cooler there and he could always teach from a boat. One evening he said to his followers, "Let us cross over to the other side of the lake." So they left the crowds and cast off the boat in which they were already sitting.

But in the middle of the night a gale blew up and the waves broke over the boat and filled it with water so that it was in danger of sinking. Meanwhile Jesus continued to sleep peacefully on a cushion at the back of the boat.

The terrified disciples went to him and woke him up. "Master, we are sinking!" they screamed. "How can you take no notice?"

So Jesus got up and he told the wind to behave itself and said to the sea, "Hush! Calm yourself". At once the wind dropped and the sea became completely smooth. Jesus turned to his companions reproachfully, "Why are you such cowards? Have you still so little faith in me?"

They were awestruck and said to each other, "What kind of man can make even the wind and sea obey him?"

By morning they had arrived at the other side of the lake in a country called Gadara. It was a desolate place, where burials took place, a stony wasteland. When Jesus stepped ashore, he was met by a wild man, naked and possessed by an evil spirit. He had been bound with iron chains but he was so strong that he broke them. No one could control him, and all day and all night long he dashed madly up and down the hillside and in the tombs, screeching and cutting himself with stones. When he saw Jesus he ran up to him and flung himself at his feet, shouting out loudly, "What do you want with me, Jesus, son of the most high God? In God's name, do not torment me!" For Jesus was already commanding the evil spirit to come out of him.

Jesus asked kindly, "What is your name?"

"My name is Legion," answered the man, "because there are so many devils inside me." And he pleaded with Jesus not to send them into outer darkness. Now there happened to be a large herd of pigs, which were animals the Jews considered unclean, feeding on the hillside and the devils begged, "Send us into the pigs!"

Jesus did as he was asked and the evil spirits fled from the man and entered the pigs. There were about two thousand of them, and the moment they felt the devils come into them, the pigs dashed straight for the cliff edge and fell into the lake and were drowned. But the man who had been mad now allowed himself to be clothed and sat down quietly in his right mind.

However, when the local people heard how he had been cured and what had happened to the pigs, they were frightened and possibly even angry, and asked Jesus to leave the district. So Jesus got back into his boat again but he wouldn't let the man who had been mad come with him. "Go home to your family and friends," he said, "and tell them what the Lord has done for you."

As soon as Jesus reached the other side of the Sea of Galilee, a huge crowd gathered round him. The head of the synagogue, whose name was Jairus, came up to him. He knelt at his feet and implored him, "My little daughter is at death's door. I beg you to lay your hands on her and make her well again."

So Jesus went along with him and the crowd came too, pressing tightly round them. Among the crowd was a woman who had suffered for many years from continual bleeding. She had spent all her money on doctors but nothing would make her better. Unseen in the mass of people, she came close to Jesus, feeling certain he could heal her. Without drawing attention to herself, she touched the hem of his tunic and at once she knew that the bleeding had stopped.

Jesus stood still and looked around, for he could feel that someone had drawn out his power of healing. He asked the disciples, "Who touched my tunic?"

"What's the use of asking," said his friends, "when you are surrounded by so many people?"

But Jesus continued to look for the person who had touched him. So the woman came forward, fearful and trembling at what she'd done. She crouched down before him and explained everything. "Daughter," responded Jesus gently, "your faith has cured you. Go in peace, freed for ever from your illness."

He was still speaking to her when a messenger came for Jairus from his home. "Your daughter is already dead", the messenger said. "There's no point in troubling the master further."

But Jesus overheard the message and told Jairus, "Do not be afraid. Have faith." And he went forward to the house, only

allowing Peter, James and John to follow him. When he arrived he found a terrific noise, with people weeping and wailing and musicians playing flutes. They were all mourning the death of the young girl.

Jesus went straight into the house and said, "Why are you making such a commotion? The girl is not dead at all; she is only sleeping." And he took the girl by the hand and said to her, "Get up, my child".

Immediately the girl, who was twelve years old, got up and began to walk about. Everybody round about could hardly believe their eyes but Jesus told them to keep quiet about it and give the girl something to eat.

ALTHOUGH Jesus performed many miracles, he spent more time talking to people and teaching them how to lead good lives. This made the Jews angry, and the Romans who ruled Israel were afraid he might want to overthrow their government. Soon after Jesus brought Jairus' daughter back to life he heard that John the Baptist, who, like him, was teaching God's message, had been killed by the Romans. His head had been chopped off.

Jesus was very sad and he took a few disciples and set sail for a deserted place on the shores of the Sea of Galilee, near Bethsaida. But the crowd wouldn't let him go so easily, and they discovered where he was going and went quickly overland so that they were waiting there when he arrived. He had no choice but to talk to them once again.

Towards the end of the afternoon, his disciples came to him and said, "This is a lonely place and it is getting late. Send the people off to the farms and villages so that they can get something to eat."

"You find them something to eat", Jesus answered.

Philip, one of his followers, asked half jokingly, "Do you expect us to go off and spend twenty pounds on bread?"

"How many loaves have you got?" Jesus asked. "Go and find out."

Another of his disciples, Andrew, came back and told him, "There is a boy here who has five barley loaves and two fishes. But what use is that among so many?"

Then Jesus told them to make the crowd sit down on the thick grass in groups, and they made up a hundred rows of fifty each. Jesus took the five loaves and two fishes; he looked up to heaven, blessed the food, broke the loaves and gave them to the disciples to distribute. He also divided the two fishes among them.

Everybody ate as much as they could, and then Jesus told them to collect the remains so that nothing should be wasted. They ended up with twelve large baskets full of scraps. Five thousand men, not including the women and children, had made a good meal.

The crowds who had seen this extraordinary miracle were so enthusiastic that they wanted to make Jesus king on the spot, but he made the disciples send the people away while he went up by himself to the mountainside where he could find a quiet place to pray.

Meanwhile the disciples got into their boat to cross back towards Capernaum. But a strong wind began to blow so hard that they couldn't use their sails and had to row. Even so they could make no headway against the huge waves.

Jesus looked across the water and saw they were in difficulties. So he went down the mountainside and walked across the sea towards them. But when the disciples saw him they were terrified and screamed out, "It's a ghost!"

Quickly Jesus reassured them, "Take heart. It is I. Don't be afraid!"

Peter called back, "Lord, if it really is you, ask me to come to you over the water."

"Come", said Jesus.

Peter stepped out of the boat and across the waves towards Jesus. But when he actually felt the wildness of the gale blowing, he was afraid and began to sink. "Lord, save me!" he shouted.

Immediately Jesus stretched out his hand and caught hold of him. "Why did you hesitate? Your belief in my power is not very strong after all."

Both of them climbed into the boat and as soon as they were safely inside, the wind dropped.

JESUS was visiting a village called Bethsaida when a blind man was brought over; he asked Jesus to lay his hands on him. Jesus took the blind man's arm and led him away out of the village. Then he spat on his eyes, laid his hands upon him and asked whether he could see anything.

The man's sight was beginning to come back. "I can see men," he said, "but they look like trees walking about."

Jesus touched his eyes again. The man looked around him very hard and this time he could see everything clearly.

So Jesus sent him home saying, "Do not tell anyone in the village."

Jesus often asked people not to spread the news of his miracles but they very seldom could resist describing such exciting events.

JESUS set off for Jerusalem and on his way he passed through the country of Samaria which was unfriendly to the Jews. As he entered a particular village, ten lepers who were outcasts because of their horrible disease, stood some way off and shouted as loud as their illness allowed them, "Jesus! Master! Have pity on us!"

When he saw them, he commanded, as if he'd already cured them, "Go off at once and show yourselves to your priests".

They went off and while they were on the way, they found the leprosy had left them and their skin was healed. One of them, finding himself cured, turned back, praising God at the top of his voice. He reached Jesus and, full of gratitude, knelt in front of him. Now he was a Samaritan and the other nine were Jews.

Jesus said to his followers, "Surely all ten were healed. But where are the other nine? Why is it that this one alone has come back to praise God and he is a foreigner?" Then Jesus turned to the Samaritan, "Get up now and go on your way. Your faith has saved you."

About two miles outside Jerusalem there's a little village called Bethany. Two sisters lived there, Martha and Mary, both of whom Jesus knew well and in whose house he had stayed. They had a brother called Lazarus who was very ill. So they sent a message to Jesus explaining that someone of whom he was fond was sick.

When Jesus received the message he said, "This illness will not lead to death but will be an example of God's wonderful ways."

Martha and Mary were told of his words but by that time Lazarus had already died.

After two days he said to his disciples, "Let us go into Judaea again."

The disciples were frightened for him. "Master," they warned him, "only recently the Jews have tried to stone you and now you're planning to go back to Jerusalem?"

Jesus answered, "Our friend Lazarus has fallen asleep but I shall go and awake him."

The disciples, thinking sleep a healthy sign, said, "Master, if he has fallen asleep he will get better."

But Jesus had meant the sleep of death. "Lazarus is dead. It is a good thing I wasn't there because what is going to happen will help you believe in me. Let us go to him now."

When Jesus arrived at Martha and Mary's house, Lazarus had already been in his tomb for four days. Many of his friends had come the short distance from Jerusalem to mourn his death. As soon as the sisters heard Jesus was on the way, Martha went out to meet him.

She said reproachfully, "If you had been here, Lord, my brother would not have died."

Jesus said, "Your brother will rise again."

"I know he will rise again on the day of judgement", Martha agreed sadly.

"I am the resurrection and life", Jesus responded, "if a man has faith in me, even if he dies, he shall come to life again. Do you believe this?"

"Lord, I do believe", replied Martha. "'I am now sure that you are the Messiah, the Son of God come down to earth."

Then Martha went to find Mary and told her quietly, "The Master is here and asking for you". So Mary hurried off to find him. The Jews who were mourning with her got up too and followed, for they assumed she was going to weep at Lazarus' tomb.

As soon as Mary reached Jesus, she fell at his feet and cried out, just as her sister had, "Oh Lord, if only you had been here my brother would not have died!"

When Jesus saw her and her companions weeping he sighed deeply and was very moved. "Where have you laid him?" he asked. They replied, "Come and see".

Jesus then began to weep too and the Jews exclaimed, "He must have loved him very much!" A few added to each other, "Why couldn't he have saved Lazarus from death? After all, he made the blind see."

Jesus heaved another deep sigh and went over to the tomb. It was a cave and the opening was sealed by a huge boulder. "Roll away the boulder", ordered Jesus.

Martha was surprised and warned him, "He has been dead four days, Lord, so he will have begun to smell."

But Jesus gave her a firm look. "Haven't I told you that if you believe strongly you will see the wonders of God?"

So they pushed aside the boulder and Jesus looked to heaven and said, "Father, I thank you for listening to me. I know you always answer my prayers, but I am speaking for the sake of the people around me so that they believe that it was you who sent me here."

Then he raised his voice, "Lazarus, come out!"

To everyone's amazement the dead man walked out, his hands and feet still bound in linen bands and his face covered with a cloth.

"Unwrap him", Jesus said. "Let him free." And that's exactly what they did. Lazarus had risen from the dead.

MOST of the people who saw Jesus perform this miracle were trustworthy and believed in him. But a few went to the Pharisees in Jerusalem and reported what he had done. The Jews were frightened because they thought he wanted to lead a revolt against their Roman rulers. So they became even more determined to kill him.

Knowing this, Jesus slipped away again and found safety at a place called Ephraim which bordered on the desert. However he knew he must die at the time God had planned for him, so when the great Jewish feast of Passover came near, he travelled to Jerusalem once more.

On his way there he stayed in Bethany with Martha and Mary and saw Lazarus, quite healthy now. The news that he was coming to Jerusalem drew an excited crowd. Even though he rode into the city on a little donkey, men, women and children lined the road to get a look at him. They threw palm leaves in front of the donkey's hooves and called out, "Hosanna, to the son of God!"

When he was surrounded by people he was safe and at night he left for Jerusalem. But at last the evening came when he was alone, praying in a garden called Gethsemane, just outside the city walls, and there he was arrested. One of his disciples, Simon Peter, was so angry that he attacked the High Priest's servant and cut off his ear with his sword.

But Jesus said, "Put away your sword. Anyone who takes up the sword will die by the sword." And then he performed his last miracle of healing and touched the servant's ear so that it was made whole again

FROM THEN on, Jesus was in captivity and performed no more miracles till after his death. He could have escaped at any time, making doors open and swords drop from the soldiers' hands. But he had chosen to die because he wanted to show his love for us.

However, he saved his greatest miracle for the end of his story on earth. On Easter morning, Jesus himself rose from the dead. It was as if all his other miracles had been preparation for this great event. Like Lazarus, he had been in the tomb for several days – although three days, not four. But no one saw him walk out, except perhaps the angel who told Mary Magdalene that he had gone. His disciples could hardly believe it when they were told the news and rushed to see the empty tomb for themselves.

But it was to Mary Magdalene that he showed himself, appearing in the person of a gardener. He said, "Woman, why are you weeping? Who are you looking for?" But still she didn't recognize him.

So he said, "Mary!" And all at once Mary Magdalene realized it was Jesus himself and she cried out joyfully, "Master!"

After Jesus had risen from the dead, he made several more miraculous appearances to his followers before he went up to heaven.